Original title:
Masonry and Metaphor

Copyright © 2024 Creative Arts Management OÜ
All rights reserved.

Author: Clement Portlander
ISBN HARDBACK: 978-9916-88-098-2
ISBN PAPERBACK: 978-9916-88-099-9

Architects of Emotion

In shadows deep, feelings play,
We shape the world in our own way.
Crafting dreams from whispered sighs,
Building castles in our eyes.

With every choice, we draw the line,
Mapping hearts where stars align.
Sculpting joy from tears we shed,
Architects of the words unsaid.

The Art of Assembling Thoughts

Fragments fall like autumn leaves,
Tangled hopes, the mind retrieves.
Colors blend in a mental throng,
Harmonizing the right from wrong.

With gentle hands, we piece together,
Words like threads in any weather.
Creating sense from chaos spun,
The art of making thoughts undone.

Cast in the Crucible

Within the heat, our spirits blaze,
Forging strength in smoldering haze.
Molding dreams that stand and fight,
Cast in the crucible's light.

From fire's kiss, new forms arise,
Resilience found in whispered cries.
Through trials faced, our souls refine,
In the crucible, we redefine.

Unearthing Secrets in Stone

Beneath the earth, tales long untold,
Whispered secrets in layers old.
Each chip reveals a story's spine,
Unearthing truths in the shifting line.

With patience worn, we carve and scrape,
In silent stones, our dreams take shape.
What lies beneath the hardened crust,
Unearthing secrets, in stone we trust.

The Alchemy of the Everyday

In morning light, shadows play,
Coffee brews in a fragrant way.
Simple acts, a magic spell,
Transform the mundane, all is well.

Walks through leaves in autumn's glow,
Every step, a tale to show.
In laughter shared, joy ignites,
Moments weave into the nights.

Rough Cuts and Fine Lines

Scarred hands shape the wood with care,
Marks of struggle left right there.
Every splinter tells a tale,
Of whispered dreams that cannot fail.

The canvas waits for strokes so bold,
Fine lines bridge the stories told.
Rough edges soften with the light,
Creation breathes as day turns night.

Bonds of the Broken

Shattered pieces, hearts entwined,
In the cracks, our souls combined.
Through the pain, we find our way,
Together forged in night and day.

With every scar, a strength we gain,
Love's resilience in the rain.
From hollow dreams, new hopes arise,
In brokenness, we find the skies.

Fragments of the Past

Dusty photos, faces fade,
Echoes whisper, memories made.
In each fragment, stories dwell,
Time's embrace, a gentle spell.

Walking paths once lost to time,
Every heartbeat, every rhyme.
History's song, we hum along,
In the past, the present strong.

The Language of Stones

Whispers of ages past, they speak,
In silence, they cradle time's embrace.
Beneath their weight, secrets seek,
    Weathered faces, each a trace.

Lithic tales in shadows cast,
Their memories etched, a silent song.
In every crack, a shadowed blast,
    History's breath carries along.

Echoes of the Past

In alleys where shadows softly creep,
Footsteps linger, stories unfold.
Through whispered winds, the echoes seep,
Voices of wanderers, brave and bold.

Memories wrought in brick and stone,
Woven in layers, thick and thin.
Each heartbeat of this world we own,
Holds the laughter, loss, and sin.

Patterns in the Dust

Footprints fading, yet they remain,
Scattered traces of tales untold.
In every grain, joy and pain,
A fleeting world, both young and old.

Swirls and lines craft wandering dreams,
Dancing shadows in evening's light.
The past is written in subtle schemes,
A tapestry of day and night.

Layers of Meaning

Beneath the surface, truths reside,
In folds of thought, lost and found.
Every layer, a place to hide,
Whispers of feelings, rich and profound.

Peeling back time, we seek to see,
The essence of life with each embrace.
In the depths, we find clarity,
A journey woven through space and grace.

Architecture of the Soul

In shadows softly cast, we rise,
With every dream, the spirit flies.
Brick by brick, our hearts align,
Creating space for love to shine.

The arches hold the weight of dreams,
The windows frame our silent screams.
Each corner tells a tale untold,
In sacred whispers, we are bold.

Foundations laid with tender care,
In this great hall, we learn to dare.
The pillars strong, they guide our way,
In the design of night and day.

As light cascades on sacred ground,
In every crack, our truth is found.
The architecture of our being,
Crafted in moments, ever freeing.

The Pivot of Possibilities

On the axis where we turn,
Dreams ignite, and passions burn.
A whispered chance can shift the fate,
In every moment, we create.

Beyond the veil of what is known,
New pathways form, sweet seeds are sown.
The horizon glows with every choice,
In silent echoes, we find our voice.

In the balance of despair and hope,
We stretch our arms, we learn to cope.
Each pivot sharp, each step we take,
Unfolding worlds, for our own sake.

The tapestry of life unwinds,
With threads of fate that fate designs.
In every twist, the heart will lead,
To realms anew, where dreams are freed.

Solid Ground Beneath Whispers

On solid ground, where secrets lie,
Beneath the stars, we breathe and sigh.
The earth supports our quiet dreams,
In tender moments, truth redeems.

Whispers travel on the breeze,
Carried gently through the trees.
In every rustle, stories flow,
Of love and loss and hearts aglow.

The roots run deep beneath our fears,
Their ancient wisdom calms our tears.
In stillness, echoes find their way,
On solid ground, we learn to stay.

As twilight wraps the world in gold,
In hushed embraces, we are bold.
The solid ground beneath our feet,
A sacred place where life's complete.

A Blueprint of the Soul

In shadows deep, the heart does dwell,
Mapping dreams, where silence fell.
Lines of longing drawn in time,
Whispers soft in rhythm's rhyme.

Crafted spaces, thoughts entwined,
Quiet hopes through space combined.
Blueprints made of pain and grace,
Sketching paths we dare to chase.

Balancing on the Edge

A tightrope stretched 'neath twilight's glow,
Each step a chance, high and low.
Courage wavers, fear takes hold,
Yet dreams ignite like stars of gold.

Caught between the rise and fall,
Every heartbeat, a daring call.
Winds of change both fierce and sweet,
Dancing lightly on this sheet.

Reconstructing the Unseen

Fragments lost, like clouds in flight,
Sculpting dreams from shards of night.
Visions blurred, yet bold we stand,
With open hearts and trembling hands.

Threads of fate, we weave anew,
Colors bright in every hue.
Building bridges from our scars,
Finding light where the shadow spars.

Mortared Memories

Brick by brick, we lay each stone,
Stories told in every tone.
Mortar mixed with laughter, tears,
Constructing walls through all the years.

Echoes linger in the night,
Flickering soft, a guiding light.
In every crack, a journey's trace,
Preserved in time, a warm embrace.

Texture of Transitions

In the dawn, shadows dance bright,
Whispers of change in morning light.
Colors blend, a soft embrace,
Life transforms, in time and space.

Leaves unfurl, new paths unwind,
Echoes of seasons, intertwined.
Fading whispers of what's been,
New horizons, freshly seen.

Raindrops fall, a gentle sigh,
Each moment's pulse, a lullaby.
Textures woven, threads of fate,
Celebrate what we create.

In twilight's glow, the world will pause,
Awaiting night with its silent cause.
Stars emerge, a whispered tune,
In transitions, we find our room.

The Canvas of Creation

With every stroke, a world unfolds,
Colors bright, and stories told.
Brush in hand, dreams take flight,
Imagining worlds in pure delight.

Swirls of chaos, patterns clear,
Artistry born from deep-seated fear.
A landscape crafted, wild and free,
Each detail sings of destiny.

Textures rich, and visions soar,
The heart knows well what it wants more.
From shades of hope to shadows cast,
Moments cherished, shadows passed.

A canvas breathes, alive with grace,
Each creation finds its place.
In art, we glimpse our hidden truth,
The canvas holds our boundless youth.

Quarried Reflections

In silent stone, a tale resides,
Carved from time where nature hides.
Each shard tells of pressure and strain,
Beauty born from ancient pain.

Luminous veins, a rugged face,
Echoes of life in their embrace.
Chiseled thoughts from depths unknown,
In quarried hearts, we find our own.

Grains of grit, rough and refined,
Seeking light that once seemed blind.
Reflecting truths through prismed light,
In every fracture, hope ignites.

From earth's embrace, a treasure found,
Silent echoes all around.
In the depths of stone, we meet,
Quarried souls, both raw and sweet.

Habitats of the Heart

In gentle nooks where love resides,
Whispers of peace in moonlit tides.
A sanctuary built on dreams,
Embracing warmth in tender seams.

Roots entwined in soil so deep,
Nurtured promises we keep.
A garden blooming, rich and rare,
In heart's habitat, we find our care.

Seasons shift, yet still we thrive,
In every pulse, our hopes alive.
Ivy hugs the weathered stone,
In sacred spaces, we're not alone.

Walls adorned with laughter's sound,
In this haven, true love is found.
Habitats of the heart, divine,
Where souls can rest, and hearts align.

Mortar Minds

In quiet rooms where thoughts collide,
Ideas form, and dreams abide.
With every word, a bridge we build,
In the silence, our hopes are filled.

Together we shape the unknown,
Crafting visions we can own.
Minds like mortar, strong and true,
Binding dreams in shades anew.

Through trials faced and laughter shared,
In this bond, we are prepared.
For every challenge, hand in hand,
We create a world, bold and grand.

With every stroke, our legacy,
Words become our symphony.
In mortar minds, we rise to fly,
Together, reaching for the sky.

Spheres of Influence

In circles drawn with gentle care,
Radiates impact, everywhere.
Whispers travel through the air,
Echoes of thoughts, beyond compare.

From heart to heart, the ripples spread,
In every mind, new paths are led.
Connections form like threads of light,
Guiding us through the dark of night.

In every sphere, a story lives,
A dance of give and take, it gives.
Influence grows, a wondrous bloom,
Filling spaces, lighting gloom.

And when we stretch beyond our time,
Our spheres entwined in sunset's rhyme.
Together made, through love's embrace,
In unity, we find our place.

Edges of Infinity

Where thoughts collide and dreams extend,
We seek the truths that never end.
At the edges, we grasp the light,
Holding visions, in endless flight.

Infinity whispers with a sigh,
Each question posed leads us to try.
In the vastness, hope remains,
Through each joy and all the pains.

We dance on borders of unknown,
In shadows cast, our courage grown.
The universe spins, weaving fate,
In the edges lies our innate.

Boundless realms in which we roam,
Each heartbeat echoing a home.
We traverse the edges, bold and free,
Infinity calls, eternally.

The Craft of Conjunctions

With each conjunction, bonds are forged,
A tapestry of life enlarged.
And, but, or—our tales entwine,
In every word, destinies align.

Crafted phrases intertwine,
Bridging hearts, through love, divine.
In simple terms, we find our way,
A union strong that will not sway.

Through common ground, support we give,
In this craft, together we live.
Joining forces, hand in hand,
We build a world, forever grand.

The craft of words, a sacred art,
In every line, we share a part.
Together, as we craft our dreams,
Conjunctions spark, igniting beams.

The Framework of Dreams

In shadows cast by whispers light,
We build the world of day and night.
Each thought a brick, each hope a beam,
Constructing life upon a dream.

With visions bright, we forge anew,
An architecture shaped by view.
The pillars stand, the rafters hum,
In every heart, a place to come.

Yet storms may strike, and doubts may rise,
A twist of fate beneath the skies.
But every crack and every seam,
Can hold the weight of fragile dreams.

So raise your voice, let courage sing,
In the framework, joy will bring.
For in the end, what shines so clear,
Are dreams we weave, year after year.

Echoes of Creation

From silence came a gentle spark,
Awakening the void so dark.
With thunderous roars, the cosmos stirred,
Each echo born, a song unheard.

The stars were sown like seeds of light,
In galaxies that dance in night.
A canvas vast, where colors blend,
In every swirl, a story penned.

Time flows on, a river clear,
Carrying whispers, far and near.
In every corner of this space,
Creation finds a sacred place.

So listen close to nature's call,
Each sound a piece, connected all.
In echoes past, our futures lie,
In every breath, we learn to fly.

Patterns of Existence

Life weaves a tapestry divine,
Where every thread, a tale aligns.
In nature's hand, a design unfolds,
In whispered winds, and stories told.

The leaves that dance in autumn's gale,
The rivers' course, the ocean's wail.
Each cycle turns, a moment's grace,
Patterns form in time and space.

In every heart, a rhythm beats,
In every soul, a truth repeats.
The web of life, both vast and small,
Is woven gently, binding all.

Finding peace in the chaos found,
In every step upon the ground.
For in the patterns we perceive,
Lies the essence of how we believe.

Heft of History

With pages worn and inked in gold,
The tales of ages, brave and bold.
Each chapter shows the rise and fall,
The weight of time, a heavy call.

From ancient lands where empires grew,
To battles fought, the struggles true.
The echoes linger, lessons learned,
In every heart, the fire burned.

Monuments stand, a solemn grace,
In stone and glass, we find our place.
Yet history flows like rivers wide,
With every turn, we learn to glide.

So carry forth the stories shared,
In every thread, the past is bared.
For in the heft of history's song,
We find our path, where we belong.

Foundations of Fragility

In whispered tones, the truth is found,
Amidst the cracks in silence profound.
Delicate threads, both weak and strong,
We build on dreams, where shadows long.

Beneath the weight, we stand so tall,
Yet fear the tremors, the slightest fall.
In every choice, a chance to cling,
To fleeting hopes, the heart will sing.

With gentle hands, we nurture grace,
In fragile spaces, we find our place.
From shattered pieces, new worlds rise,
In the soft light, our spirits fly.

So here we stand, on wobbly ground,
Hearing the echoes of life's sound.
Foundations built on dreams so bright,
We dance through darkness, into the light.

The Harmony of Hardships

In struggles faced, a melody,
A symphony of pain set free.
Each note a lesson, harsh yet clear,
In trials met, we find our cheer.

With heavy hearts, we learn to rise,
In every storm, a hidden prize.
Resilience blooms where roots grow deep,
In hard-fought battles, promises keep.

Embrace the discord, find the tune,
Through darkest nights, we seek the moon.
Every setback is a step toward light,
In hardships' dance, we take our flight.

The harmony of life unfolds,
With strength in weakness, we are bold.
Together we sing, through joy and strife,
In the chorus of this precious life.

Vaulted Dreams

In twilight hours, dreams take flight,
Beneath the stars, in veils of light.
Each whispered wish, a soaring arc,
A canvas vast, we leave our mark.

With every heartbeat, hopes ignite,
In the stillness, they shine so bright.
Like birds in flight, unbound, we soar,
Chasing vistas we long to explore.

Through valleys low and mountains high,
We carve our paths, we learn to fly.
In vaulted skies, our spirits gleam,
We rise together, on currents of dream.

So let us reach for heights unknown,
In unity, we find our own.
With every leap, we touch the stars,
In vaulted dreams, we are never far.

The Quarry of Ideas

In the quarry deep, thoughts take shape,
Chiseling wonders, a myriad drape.
From granite minds, ideas flow,
A treasure trove, where insights glow.

Each notion sparked, a stone of gold,
In the hands of dreamers, they unfold.
Tools of vision, sharp and clear,
We sculpt the future, year by year.

With every strike, a vision grows,
In shadows cast, creativity flows.
The quarry thrives, it never sleeps,
In the heart of thinkers, passion leaps.

So gather round, let voices rise,
In the quarry of thought, wisdom lies.
Together we'll carve new paths to tread,
With every idea, the world is fed.

The Language of Load-Bearing

In silence, we carry unseen weight,
Words lift heavy thoughts, create.
Structures of doubt and dreams collide,
In our hearts, they abide.

With every spoken phrase, we strive,
To bridge the gaps, keep hope alive.
Load-bearing beams of trust remain,
Through joy and through pain.

Beneath the burden, spirits rise,
In shared stories, friendship flies.
Together we stand, side by side,
In this journey, we confide.

The bricks we build make us strong,
In unity, we all belong.
Crafting a language, bold and clear,
To face our burdens without fear.

Crafting Realities

From thoughts to forms, our hands create,
Dreams shaped in clay, they resonate.
With every twist, the future bends,
Crafting worlds where vision extends.

Artisans of moments, we design,
A tapestry of lives intertwine.
Each stroke a story, rich and deep,
In the silence, secrets keep.

Through trials and triumphs, we refine,
The essence of our truths align.
In the studio of hope, we find,
New beginnings, paths combined.

Reality shifts with every touch,
We mold the fabric, loved so much.
Crafting the spaces, bright and new,
Where all desires can come true.

Balancing the Unknown

In the quiet, we feel the sway,
Of futures dark, clouds of gray.
Walking the line, we hesitate,
Finding strength in what awaits.

With every step, the fear may rise,
Yet in the dark, our courage flies.
Embracing risk, we learn to dance,
To take a leap, to seize the chance.

In the void, creation thrives,
Balancing dreams as hope survives.
Through the chaos, we find our way,
The unknown holds a bright array.

Trust the journey, let it flow,
In uncertainty, learn to grow.
Weaving the threads of fate's design,
In the mystery, hearts align.

Sweeping Away the Ruins

Among the ashes, we start anew,
With every breath, life breaks through.
Sweeping away the past's decay,
To find the strength for a brighter day.

The remnants whisper of what once was,
Stories linger without applause.
Yet in the rubble, seeds are sown,
In grief, the heart learns to atone.

With careful hands, we clear the space,
Creating a home, a warm embrace.
From every sorrow, lessons gleaned,
In the silence, hope convened.

Together we rise, hearts ablaze,
Building tomorrows in endless ways.
Sweeping the ruins, we find the light,
In every ending, a new insight.

Shadows in Mortar

In the cracks where sunlight fades,
Whispers dance in dusk's embrace.
Footsteps echo on old charades,
Memories wear a timeless face.

Moss-covered stones keep secrets tight,
Echos of laughter haunt the lane.
With each twilight, the world feels right,
Yet shadows linger, whispering pain.

Underneath the rusted beams,
Dreams inhabit dusty halls.
In silence, life unravels seams,
Where history's curtain gently falls.

Ghosts of love and loss collide,
In every shadow, every sigh.
The past and present intertwine,
As echoes fade but never die.

The Structure of Sentiments

In beams of hope, we lay our dreams,
With every nail, we stake our claim.
Framing moments, stitched at seams,
    Crafting love within this frame.

Windows wide to let in grace,
Doors swing open to the heart.
In every corner, we find a trace,
    Of the beauty in love's art.

Hearts constructed with each smile,
Strengthened by the tears we've shed.
Together we can bridge each mile,
    Building walls where love is fed.

Cementing trust with every stone,
    In the foundation, we reside.
In this structure, we're not alone,
For love is where our dreams abide.

Building Bridges of Silence

In quiet halls where echoes dwell,
We construct paths of unspoken words.
Every glance tells a gentle tale,
Where thoughts take flight like migrating birds.

Bridges built on muted sighs,
Connecting hearts on either side.
In the stillness, our truth lies,
A sacred bond, our spirits guide.

The weight of silence, heavy yet light,
Forms the foundation of knowing hearts.
Each moment cherished, pure delight,
A bridge where love forever starts.

As shadows fade to the softest glow,
The fabric of silence weaves our fate.
In the quiet, our love will grow,
Building bridges where souls create.

Chiseling the Heart

With gentle hands, we carve our dreams,
Sculpting love from marble's core.
Each stroke reveals what nature means,
A masterpiece we both adore.

Chiseling away the rough and raw,
Finding beauty in every flaw.
Emotions shaped with tender care,
Creating art beyond compare.

Fractured pieces join to form,
A vessel of strength that can endure.
In the fire of hearts, we transform,
With love, we etch our lives for sure.

Each chisel tap, a rhythmic dance,
Crafting moments that intertwine.
In every heartbeat, a second chance,
Chiseling the heart, a love divine.

The Labor of Letters

In shadows cast by ink and quill,
Each word a climb, a steady will.
Beneath the weight of silent thoughts,
A symphony where meaning's caught.

With each stroke, a story weaves,
The heart's confessions, art believes.
Fragmented dreams in black and white,
Turn whispered hopes to blazing light.

The canvas rich, yet bare of sight,
A dance of letters, bold and bright.
In every pause, a breath profound,
The labor of love in silence found.

Ode to those, who dare to write,
To chisel truths from darkest night.
With every line, creation thrives,
The labor of letters ever strives.

Mortar Between the Lines

In spaces soft, where silence breathes,
The mortar binds our thoughts and dreams.
Between each line, stories entwine,
A hidden strength in what defines.

The gaps we leave are filled with light,
Each breath suspended, day and night.
In whispered tones, the secrets lie,
The unspoken truths we can't deny.

Each pause a bridge, a chance to see,
The world beyond, the 'you' and 'me.'
In the stillness, we find our way,
The mortar's grip in texts that sway.

Unseen but felt, the ties that hold,
In every tale, the warmth unfold.
Beyond the words, the heart aligns,
With care, we craft the mortar lines.

Textures of Time

In fleeting moments, shadows dance,
The texture soft, a whispered chance.
Each second layered, richly spun,
In patterns drawn, we come undone.

Grains of sand through fingers slide,
Against our will, they shift and hide.
The tapestry of life unfurls,
In vibrant hues, our story swirls.

Seasons weave in threads of gold,
With every turn, new tales unfold.
A fabric strong, yet delicate,
The textures blend, we speculate.

In every thread, our histories,
Woven close in soft reveries.
Embrace the moments, let them rhyme,
For in each breath, the textures climb.

The Pillars of Perception

In minds awake, the pillars rise,
Constructed firm, they touch the skies.
With every thought, a beam of light,
Defining worlds in day and night.

The lens we wear, a frame refined,
Shapes the visions we design.
Through cracks of doubt, the visions flow,
With wisdom's grace, our spirits grow.

Each pillar stands, both strong and free,
A testament to what we see.
In shadows cast by past and dream,
We build our truth, a shared esteem.

The heart ignites with every gaze,
Transforming darkness into praise.
In columns tall, we find our voice,
The pillars of perception, choice.

The Artisan's Dream

In twilight's glow, the craftsman wakes,
With gentle hands, his spirit quakes.
A world of shapes beneath his tools,
Whispers of beauty amidst the rules.

His heart a canvas, colors blend,
With each small stroke, his thoughts ascend.
Dreams carved in wood, in stone refined,
In every piece, a story entwined.

The sound of chisels, a rhythmic song,
Echoes softly where they belong.
With love and patience, he carves his fate,
In shadows and light, he dreams, awaits.

A final touch, the moment near,
The craft alive, the vision clear.
His dream unfolds, in silence gleams,
The artisan's heart, woven in dreams.

Walls of Whispered Wisdom

Within these walls, the tales reside,
Ancient echoes where secrets hide.
Each crack and crevice holds a thought,
Lessons learned, and battles fought.

The stories linger in every stone,
Wisdom shared, never alone.
Whispers travel on the air,
Of lives well-lived and hearts laid bare.

In quiet moments, we pause and hear,
The voices carried year by year.
These walls, a guardian, a silent guide,
Embrace our fears as they subside.

A tapestry of voices, warm and bright,
Guiding us through the longest night.
Within these walls, we come to learn,
That wisdom shines, like flickering burn.

Chisel and Charcoal

With chisel and charcoal, dreams take flight,
Shapes emerge from the heart of night.
Soft lines drawn on forgotten slate,
A dance of shadows that captivate.

The artist's breath, a steady stream,
In every stroke, a whispered dream.
Charcoal smudges, like memories blur,
Life captured in lines that softly stir.

Carved out moments, expressions bold,
Stories etched that must be told.
A chisel bites, a heart laid bare,
In charcoal hues, the world we share.

A page of black, a canvas wide,
The artist's soul, his endless pride.
With every mark, the journey's true,
In chisel's dance, all dreams renew.

The Structure of Solitude

In solitude's embrace, I find my space,
A quiet realm, a gentle grace.
Amidst the silence, thoughts take form,
Building dreams in the calmest storm.

Each brick of quiet, a shielded wall,
Protects my heart, allows me to fall.
In shadows cast by my own design,
A sanctuary where I align.

The structure stands, both firm and free,
A haven where I can simply be.
With every breath, I carve my way,
Through endless night into the day.

In this solitude, creativity flows,
Like wildflowers in forgotten rows.
A sacred space where I am whole,
The structure of solitude, my soul's console.

Echoing Wallflower

In gardens where the whispers dwell,
A wallflower blooms, a silent bell.
With colors bright, it hides away,
Its fragrance soft, a muted play.

It watches dreams as shadows glide,
In sunlight's glow, it takes no pride.
Yet in the night, it softly sighs,
As whispered secrets touch the skies.

The world around, a bustling stream,
Yet it remains, a gentle dream.
With every breeze, it sways and leans,
A quiet witness to what seems.

Though often lost, it holds its ground,
In solitude, beauty is found.
The wallflower stands, a heart so true,
A whispering soul in every hue.

Pillars of Intuition

On rocky peaks, where shadows play,
Stand pillars strong, come what may.
They listen close to nature's call,
With silent strength, they will not fall.

Through storms that rage, they hold their post,
Guardians of wisdom, never lost.
Their silent watch, a guiding star,
In every heart, they show us far.

With roots that dig into the earth,
They nurture dreams, give hope its birth.
In stillness, they embrace the air,
And whisper truths that few can share.

These pillars stand, both bold and wise,
Reflecting light from azure skies.
In quiet moments, trust their sway,
For they know paths where shadows stray.

Foundations Beneath the Surface

Beneath the waves, where silence reigns,
Foundations lie, captured in chains.
They breathe the weight of time and tide,
In hidden depths, where secrets hide.

The currents shift, the sands will creep,
While ancient whispers softly seep.
What lies below, a world unknown,
In darkened halls, the past has grown.

Yet every stone, a story tells,
Of laughter, tears, and hidden spells.
With roots entwined, they hold the ground,
A tapestry of life, profound.

In still reflection, truth reveals,
The strength in shadows, the heart that heals.
Foundations firm, though out of sight,
They cradle dreams, igniting light.

Crafting the Invisible

With nimble hands, the artist weaves,
A tapestry that none perceives.
In whispers soft, the colors blend,
To shape the world, create, transcend.

Each stroke a breath, a silent song,
Creating realms where hearts belong.
Though seen by few, their essence flows,
In secret gardens, magic grows.

Beyond the eye, the spirit roams,
In shadows deep, it finds its homes.
Crafting dreams, the unseen glide,
Through every heart, their paths abide.

With patience true, they mold the air,
Transforming thoughts into a prayer.
For in the quiet, the magic spurs,
Crafting the invisible in hers.

Spires of the Imagination

Reaching high into the sky,
Whispers of dreams drift by.
Colors splash on canvas bright,
In the depths of endless night.

Thoughts like birds begin to soar,
Chasing shadows to explore.
Crafting visions, brick by brick,
With each heartbeat, we create, tick.

Echoes ring in silent halls,
Where the mind's great journey calls.
Spires rise with every breath,
Building stories that defy death.

In the realms where wonders blend,
Imagination knows no end.
Every thought a sacred spark,
Illuminating paths so dark.

The Geometry of Hope

In angles sharp, we find our way,
Through lines of light, we choose to stay.
Each corner turned holds promise dear,
As shadows fade and dreams appear.

Shapes that dance in endless space,
Give rise to hope and gentle grace.
Circles close, yet never bind,
In every edge, new paths we find.

Triangles form a sturdy base,
Building strength with every trace.
From vertices, our spirits climb,
Forging futures, one step at a time.

The geometry, a bright design,
In hearts where hope and love entwine.
With every part, life finds its plan,
In every soul, the spark of man.

Labyrinths of Reflection

Paths twist and turn, a silent maze,
In mirrors deep, where time can gaze.
Every corner harbors thought,
Lessons learned, and battles fought.

Whispers echo against the wall,
Guiding footsteps through the hall.
In shadows cast, the light will shine,
Illuminating the heart's design.

Each turn reveals a story told,
Of hopes and fears both brave and bold.
In the depths of winding ways,
We uncover the truth that stays.

Labyrinths, both fierce and kind,
Holding secrets of the mind.
Through woven paths, we come to see,
The reflection of what must be.

Foundations Beneath the Surface

Roots entwined in silent earth,
Whispers soft of nature's birth.
Hidden strength in every layer,
A testament to life's prayer.

Beneath the ground, the stories lie,
Of all who lived, and dared to try.
Foundations strong, yet often unseen,
Build the dreams of what has been.

The pulse of life runs deep and true,
In rich soil, both old and new.
Nurtured by the winds of change,
In every heart, we rearrange.

When storms arise and skies turn gray,
The roots below will guide the way.
Foundations firm, in peace, we stand,
Connected all, by nature's hand.

Buried Treasures of Thought

In the quiet corners, secrets lie,
Whispers of dreams that once aimed high.
Lost in the sands of time's embrace,
Glimmers of truth in a hidden space.

Beneath the surface, treasures gleam,
Fragments of hope, lost in a dream.
Each thought a jewel, waiting to shine,
A tapestry woven, yours and mine.

Dare to dig deep in the fertile ground,
Cherish the silence, hear the sound.
Moments forgotten, yet still they breathe,
In the garden of thought, we weave and weave.

Uncover the riches within your soul,
Embrace the journey, let it console.
For buried treasures await your find,
In the heart's labyrinth, gentle and kind.

Shadows in the Deconstruction

In the ruins of what was once whole,
Shadows dance on the fragments of soul.
Piece by piece, we begin to see,
Life's beautiful chaos setting us free.

Walls that echoed tales of despair,
Now whisper secrets of how to repair.
Each crack a story, each crumble a chance,
In the night's silence, the shadows prance.

Rebuild the light from these scattered parts,
Mend the fractures, awaken the hearts.
In the dark corners, hope still thrives,
Shadows in deconstruction, love survives.

From the ashes of pain, we shall rise,
Crafting new visions with open eyes.
In the dance of decay, beauty spins,
In the shadows, the journey begins.

Masons of Memory

With each brick laid, a story unfolds,
Crafted with laughter, with tears, with gold.
Masons of memory, building the past,
Foundations of wisdom, meant to last.

Carved in the stone are moments we've shared,
Heartfelt whispers of those who have cared.
In the structure of time, we find our way,
Guided by memories, come what may.

The archways of life, they bend and sway,
Each passage leads us to yesterday.
A fortress of feelings, strong and true,
In the masons' hands, the old turns new.

As we add layers, both thick and thin,
We treasure the tales of where we've been.
For in every crack, a legacy stays,
Masons of memory, weaving our days.

The Prism of Legacy

Through the prism, our lives break apart,
Colors of history, blending in art.
Each hue a story, vibrant and bright,
Legacy shines in the depths of the night.

Fractured reflections of those who've passed,
Their dreams and hopes forever amassed.
In the spectrum, we find our place,
Embracing our roots, our shared grace.

Moments refracted, dancing in light,
Guiding the future, igniting the night.
With every whisper, they call to us still,
In the prism of legacy, we find our will.

Together we stand on the shoulders of time,
Crafting tomorrow in rhythm and rhyme.
For in every facet, a truth we embrace,
The prism of legacy, our sacred space.

Echoes in the Stone

Whispers of time, in silence they shout,
Ancient tales carved, of shadows and doubt.
Beneath heavy layers, their stories reside,
In the heart of the earth, where secrets abide.

Molds of forgotten, in granite and clay,
Erosion of memories, drifting away.
Yet, listen closely, the echoes remain,
Beckoning souls to discover the pain.

Each crack in the surface, a testament told,
Of love and of loss, of warmth turned to cold.
With every touch, the past lingers long,
In the depths of the stone, we find where we belong.

So stand by the rock, let your spirit roam,
In whispers of stone, you'll find your way home.

Building Bridges with Words

Words like bricks, laid with care,
Building a bridge, spanning despair.
Each syllable crafted, strong and precise,
Connecting two hearts, a delicate slice.

Crafted in silence, yet loud as a roar,
Voices unite, letting spirits soar.
Across the divide, like beams of pure light,
Words weave the darkness, bringing the bright.

From whispers to shouts, they carry our dreams,
In the tapestry woven, hope gently gleams.
With every step forward, the distance now shrinks,
In the bridge of our making, the world softly blinks.

So gather your letters, let stories unfold,
In the heart of connection, we find what we hold.

Crafting a New Narrative

In the shadows of doubt, a new tale is spun,
With ink on the page, where old fears are done.
Pages unturned, the past held at bay,
In the ink of tomorrow, we find our own way.

Carving each chapter with passion and grace,
Unraveling truths we once dared not face.
With courage we stand, our stories take flight,
In the depths of our hearts, we embrace the light.

Lines that entwine, like threads intertwined,
Creating a fabric, a purpose defined.
With every new stanza, we learn and we grow,
In the narrative written, our spirits flow.

So craft your own story, let it be bold,
In the book of your life, let your voice be told.

Sculpted Moments

In the marble of time, memories breed,
Sculpted with tenderness, shattering speed.
Chiseled with care, each moment a piece,
In the gallery of life, we find our release.

Shapes of experience, both joy and despair,
Crafted by choices, the weight we all bear.
With every breath drawn, a sculpture refined,
In the canvas of days, our essence combined.

Motion immortalized, in stillness we find,
Echoes of laughter, a tapestry blind.
Moments that shimmer, in light they ignite,
Turning fleeting glimpses into pure delight.

So cherish the seconds, let each one be known,
For the art of our lives is collectively grown.

Fragments of a Broken Narrative

Whispers linger in the air,
Promises made, now unaware.
Scattered thoughts, like leaves in fall,
Echoes fade; we feel them all.

A story told in shattered bits,
Each moment holds what hope permits.
Time rewinds and then reframes,
Loss surrounds, but still it claims.

Pictures hang on empty walls,
Faded ink, the silence calls.
In the cracks, the truth resides,
Memory's grip, a silent tide.

Between the lines, we try to find,
The pieces left, so intertwined.
In the quiet, understanding grows,
A broken tale that softly glows.

Designed in Silence

In stillness lies a gentle force,
An architect of whispered course.
Thoughts converge in tranquil space,
Molding dreams with perfect grace.

The canvas waits for strokes of night,
As shadows weave their softest light.
Silhouettes dance upon the ground,
In silence, art and heart surround.

Echoes stir in midnight's breath,
Crafting secrets, life, and death.
Through the hush, intentions bloom,
In quiet halls, we find our room.

Each moment etched, a silent song,
Where solitude and strength belong.
Designed in silence, we create,
An inner world that resonates.

Cementing Connections

Bricks of trust form sturdy walls,
Binding hearts where silence calls.
Hands are joined in shared intent,
Building dreams, a firm ascent.

Through storms we weave our tapestry,
Strengthened by our history.
Each laughter shared, each tear embraced,
Cementing bonds that time cannot erase.

Paths aligned beneath the moon,
Together hum our cherished tune.
In every glance, a promise made,
Connections forged, never to fade.

With every step, the journey grows,
In unity, resilience shows.
Cementing paths with love and light,
Together, we reach for new heights.

Carved Verses

In the bark of ancient trees,
Whispers flow with every breeze.
Words engraved like seeds of thought,
Nature speaks what life has taught.

Carved verses in the stone,
Stories shared, no longer lone.
Echoes of the past remain,
In the grains, the joy and pain.

Ink and stone, a fusion rare,
Each letter shaped with tender care.
Poems live where souls collide,
In every mark, a heart's true guide.

From simple lines to verses grand,
Art and life, a woven band.
Carved verses speak from deep within,
Telling tales where we have been.

Pathways of the Mind

In corridors of thought we roam,
Each twist and turn leads us home.
Ideas flicker like fireflies,
Illuminating the darkest skies.

Through winding paths of dreams we trace,
A tapestry of time and space.
We gather whispers, soft yet bold,
A treasure trove of stories told.

In a labyrinth of hopes and fears,
We navigate through laughter and tears.
Every step, a dance with fate,
In the heart of the mind, we await.

As stars align in the night sky,
We find the strength to learn to fly.
With open hearts, we seek and find,
The endless pathways of the mind.

Tracing Shadows on Mortar

On ancient walls, where stories blend,
We trace the shadows that never end.
Mortar binds the past to now,
Each crack a tale, we wonder how.

The sunlight dances on the stones,
Resonating with whispered tones.
Every shadow wears a face,
History's echo, time's embrace.

We walk the paths where moments lay,
In silence, they have much to say.
A canvas of memory, rich and deep,
In the heart of mortar, secrets sleep.

As dusk descends, the shadows grow,
Each whispering story starts to flow.
Tracing shadows, hand in hand,
We honor the past, where we stand.

Archways to the Unknown

Beneath the archways, dreams take flight,
Into the realms of day and night.
Each passage leads to lands unseen,
Where secrets whisper and hearts convene.

The arches rise like hopes anew,
Inviting souls to wander through.
With every step, we break the mold,
In the unknown, we weave the bold.

In shadows cast by flickering light,
We find the courage to ignite.
The pathway stretches, vast and wide,
An open door, let's walk inside.

With open arms, we greet the dawn,
Across the threshold, fears are gone.
Archways beckon, let's explore,
The unknown whispers, evermore.

Rough Hands, Polished Ideas

With rough hands calloused by the toil,
We turn the earth, we sow the soil.
Ideas bloom like flowers bright,
Nurtured in the morning light.

In every scratch, a story lives,
Of dreams we chase and hope we give.
Polished bright by sweat and tears,
Crafted through the trials of years.

We build the future with every nail,
Against the odds, we shall not fail.
Rough hands carry visions grand,
Holding fast to what we've planned.

In the garden of our minds, we see,
How roughness shapes our destiny.
Polished ideas, shining true,
Born from labor, made anew.

A Tapestry of Stones

In quiet corners, shadows play,
Fragmented dreams, in disarray.
Each pebble whispers tales untold,
A history rich, both brave and bold.

Colors blend beneath soft skies,
An mosaic where beauty lies.
Nature's craft, with patience sewn,
A tapestry of stones, alone.

Worn by time, yet strong they stand,
Each one placed with steady hand.
Together forming paths we tread,
In silent strength, their wisdom spread.

In every crack, a story speaks,
Each facet glints, as sunlight seeks.
A journey forged in earth and time,
A gift of nature, pure and sublime.

Hidden Charms in Rough Edges

Beneath the surface, beauty hides,
In every crag where light abides.
A whispered breeze, a secret song,
In rugged hearts, where dreams belong.

The jagged cuts may seem unkind,
Yet treasures wait, for those who find.
Embrace the flaws, let them unfold,
For gems are born from stories told.

Each rough edge tells of battles fought,
Of lessons learned and love distraught.
The charm within the tear-streaked stone,
Is worth the weight of being alone.

In twilight's glow, with tender grace,
We celebrate this sacred space.
For hidden charms, though hard to see,
Make life a rich tapestry.

The Weight of Expression

Words fall heavy on fragile ears,
Carrying burdens of unspoken fears.
In syllables wrapped in soft disguise,
A heart laid bare, it humbly cries.

The ink flows thick with whispered pain,
In silent moments, love's refrain.
Each stroke a weight, both dark and light,
Revealing truths within the night.

Expressions dance on paper thin,
A canvas where the soul begins.
To speak is to bleed, to share is to mend,
In every story, we find a friend.

Yet silence holds a world of its own,
In quiet reverie, seeds are sown.
The weight of words can lift or break,
In every choice, the heart must quake.

Silenced Scribes

In darkened halls where echoes fade,
The silent scribes their secrets laid.
With quills held tight and ink spent dry,
They pen their truths beneath the sky.

Lost in shadows, their voices blend,
With tales of woe and love's sweet mend.
Each line a thread of life and lore,
A history written to implore.

Yet whispers linger, held afar,
In every heart a hidden star.
For even silence has a sound,
In every pause, the world unbound.

As pages turn and eras shift,
These silenced scribes their words still gift.
In quiet corners, stories gleam,
Awakening the past from dream.

The Weight of Inspiration

In the quiet night, a whisper calls,
Dreams weave through the shadows of the walls.
A flicker of hope, under the stars,
Illuminates paths, how near, how far.

Like heavy stones, ideas rest,
Pressed down with longing in the chest.
Yet with each breath, they rise anew,
Balancing weight with the heart's true hue.

Inspiration strikes like lightning's flash,
Filling the void, a brilliant splash.
Hold onto visions, they fade so fast,
Capture the moment, make it last.

So let the muse guide your steady hand,
Navigate dreams, like grains of sand.
The weight transforms into a light crown,
Wear it with pride, never back down.

Fragments of the Heart

Splintered pieces scattered wide,
Each shard holds a tale, a hidden guide.
Moments cherished, echoes that sing,
Fragments of love, what joy they bring.

In the depth of sorrow, we find our grace,
Picking up pieces we dare to face.
Healing begins when we start to see,
The beauty in scars, the strength to be free.

Whispers of laughter, shadows of tears,
Combined they form the essence of years.
Collect the fragments, let them inspire,
Building anew from the ashes of fire.

Every heartbeat echoes past's embrace,
In every fragment, a sacred place.
Dance with the pieces, weave them like art,
For life is a canvas—the heart is the start.

Stones of Thought

Stones align in a winding path,
Each a thought, a gentle math.
Gathering wisdom, one by one,
Carve out a journey, 'til day is done.

Smooth as pebbles, rough as fate,
Thoughts meander at their own rate.
Tumbled by time, they find their voice,
In the quiet moments, make their choice.

With every step, they teach us grace,
Transforming pain into time and space.
Stack them high or lay them low,
Each stone a lesson, a place to grow.

So tread the path with open mind,
Leave no stone unturned, no thought confined.
For in every rock, a story hides,
A spark of truth where wisdom abides.

Foundations of the Imagination

In shadows deep, ideas take flight,
Foundations whisper in the dead of night.
Crafting dreams from dust and air,
Building visions, laid with care.

A spark ignites, a canvas awaits,
Colors swirl through the open gates.
Imagination blooms like spring's first flower,
Each petal a thought, its vibrant power.

From roots of hope, creativity grows,
In unexplored lands, the spirit flows.
Lay down the bricks of vision and trust,
For in the mind's realm, there's magic to dust.

So raise your hands to the sky's embrace,
Construct your future, find your place.
In the foundations, let dreams expand,
For imagination is our strongest hand.

The Craft of Connection

In the weave of a smile, we share a thread,
Threads of laughter, where hopes are spread.
In the warmth of a touch, hearts intertwine,
In the quiet of moments, new ties align.

Listen close to the whispers, they sing,
A melody of memories, sweet and ring.
In the garden of friendship, seeds softly sown,
With nurturing care, love has grown.

Bridges built with patience, with hands so kind,
Uniting our stories, our hearts intertwined.
In every shared glance, a promise unfolds,
A treasure of trust, more precious than gold.

So craft this connection, with thoughtful intent,
In the tapestry of life, let love be the scent.
With every shared heartbeat, we find our way,
In the art of connection, forever we'll stay.

Erecting Walls of Memory

In the corners of mind, the echoes reside,
Steadfast and strong, where whispers abide.
Each brick is a moment, each stone a tale,
Erecting this structure, though time may pale.

The laughter once shared, now ghosts in the air,
Soft shadows of yesteryear linger with care.
Windows wide open, to let sunlight in,
Yet behind these tall walls, is where dreams begin.

Carved into the plaster, the names we once wrote,
On the surface of time, nostalgia will float.
These walls stand resilient, against the strange tide,
Holding close to the warmth where our memories hide.

So cherish the walls, rise steadfast and proud,
In the heart of the builder, all is allowed.
Erecting the memories, stone by stone,
In the tapestry of life, we're never alone.

The Geometry of Dreams

In the angles of night, where starlight aligns,
Shapes of our dreams dance, in delicate signs.
Circles of visions that spiral and glide,
In the map of our souls, we take a wild ride.

Triangles form, creating the path,
As we chase our desires, escaping the wrath.
With each measured step, towards horizons anew,
We sketch our ambitions, in vibrant hues too.

Rectangles of hope invite growth and a plan,
Filling spaces of silence, in the life we began.
In the canvas of night, the patterns unfold,
The geometry of dreams, in stories retold.

So navigate boldly, with heart as your guide,
In the realms of the dreamers, let courage reside.
With lines intersecting, in unity's beam,
We discover our purpose, the geometry of dreams.

The Way of the Trowel

With the trowel in hand, we shape and we mold,
Crafting our visions, both gentle and bold.
Layer upon layer, we build from the ground,
In the soil of our hearts, a haven is found.

Each stroke tells a story, of effort and care,
As we smooth out the edges, and paint with the air.
In the rhythm of motion, creation comes alive,
With every small push, our passions will thrive.

In the patience of time, the masterpiece grows,
With each careful choice, our artistry shows.
For in the act of crafting, the spirit awakes,
The path of the trowel, in joy it makes.

So let's wield our tools, with purpose and pride,
In the journey of crafting, together we'll stride.
For the way of the trowel, is where dreams take flight,
In the canvas of life, we'll paint it so bright.

Sculpting the Void

In silence deep, the void does breathe,
A canvas bare, where dreams may weave.
Shapes emerge from whispered thoughts,
As shadows dance, reality is sought.

With careful hands, the formless found,
In empty space, new worlds abound.
Each stroke a prayer, each line a sigh,
Carving the silence, we learn to fly.

Echoes rise from depths unknown,
In sculpted air, the heart is shown.
We mold our fears into the night,
And find our souls in echoes bright.

Thus the void, no longer stark,
Blooms into life, igniting spark.
A masterpiece from absence made,
In sculpting voids, our truths displayed.

Signposts of Existence

Beneath the stars, we search for signs,
Each path we tread, through tangled pines.
Moments marked by joy and pain,
In shadows cast, our truths remain.

Every heartbeat, a whispered guide,
In the labyrinth where dreams collide.
With every choice, a path unveils,
Signposts shining through the gales.

From childhood's laugh to elder's sigh,
We navigate as days go by.
Through twisting roads, in light and dark,
We leave behind our gentle mark.

Gathering tales like autumn leaves,
In the tapestry that life weaves.
In the end, it is love that leads,
The signposts found in timeless deeds.

The Artisan's Lament

In quiet hours, the artisan toils,
With hands worn rough, amidst the spoils.
Crafting dreams from clay and fire,
Each creation born of deep desire.

Yet in the stillness, shadows creep,
A nagging doubt disturbs his sleep.
Is beauty lost in the striving hand?
Or does it rise as he dreams and stands?

With every stroke, a story spun,
Of battles fought, and victories won.
But what if the heart cannot express,
The aching depths of its own distress?

He weaves lament into each piece,
Informed by sorrows, searching for peace.
An artisan's heart, both strong and frail,
In every crack, there rests a tale.

In the Grip of Time

Time holds tight, a relentless chase,
Moments slip in a silent race.
Each tick a whisper, each tock a sigh,
As days cascade and years comply.

Memories etched in fragile dust,
In the sands of fate, we place our trust.
We grasp the now, yet watch it fade,
In the grip of time, our choices made.

Every glance backward, a chance to learn,
In the fire of past, we burn and churn.
Yet forward we march, through thick and thin,
In the dance of life, we lose and win.

Time, the sculptor of who we become,
With tender strokes, we play the drum.
In every heartbeat, we find our rhyme,
Embracing the beauty in the grip of time.

Ties That Anchor

In the depths of the sea, we find our way,
Bound by the whispers of tides at play.
Ropes intertwined, a bond so tight,
Holding us steady, through day and night.

In stormy weather, we stand as one,
Facing the chaos, we will not run.
The ties that anchor, sturdy and true,
Guide us onward, steadfast in view.

With every wave that crashes near,
We find our strength, we conquer fear.
Together we rise, unbroken and bold,
Stories of love and courage unfold.

So here we sail, on this vast sea,
With ties that anchor, we are free.
Through tempests and calm, our hearts align,
In each other's arms, forever we shine.

The Craft of Inner Landscapes

In quiet corners of the mind's embrace,
Hidden vistas bloom, a sacred space.
Colors of memories blend and collide,
Painting the canvas, where dreams abide.

The brush strokes of thought, gentle and wise,
Crafting horizons beneath sunlit skies.
Mountains of wonder rise tall and grand,
Rivers of feeling flow through the land.

Whispers of silence dance through the trees,
Echoing secrets carried by the breeze.
In the heart's garden, each petal awakes,
Creating a haven, where stillness breaks.

So wander these paths, where shadows are cast,
Discover the beauty of the present and past.
In the craft of landscapes, both inner and true,
Find the light that shines just for you.

Chiseled Ciphers

Etched in stone, the stories unfold,
Chiseled ciphers, whispers of old.
Symbols and signs, a timeless embrace,
Carved into earth, a sacred space.

Each line tells a tale of ages gone by,
An echo of hearts that dared to fly.
Between the cracks, a journey appears,
Transcending the silence, through laughter and tears.

With every chisel strike, the past comes alive,
Breathing in secrets, where legends derive.
The echoes of mortals, their hopes and their fears,
Captured in time, throughout the years.

So pause and ponder these ciphers aglow,
The wisdom they hold, the truth they bestow.
In stone, we find pieces of who we are,
Chiseled eternally, our dreams reach afar.

The Solace of Structure

In the arms of order, we find our ground,
The solace of structure, profound and sound.
Each line and corner, a pattern of grace,
Holding the chaos, a quiet embrace.

Bridges of reason span the divides,
Mapping the journey where purpose resides.
Architecture of life, both simple and grand,
Creating a framework, a steady hand.

With every foundation, a story begins,
The rhythms of being, where growth never ends.
In harmony crafted, we learn how to thrive,
Within the confines, our spirits alive.

So cherish the moments where structure is found,
In the ebb and flow of what life surrounds.
With every design, our paths intertwine,
In the solace of structure, our hearts align.

Stone by Stone

In the quiet dusk, stones gather round,
Each one a whisper, a silent sound.
Layer by layer, we build our way,
As time's gentle hands shape the clay.

Each stone a story, each crack a line,
Worn by the seasons, weathered by time.
Held by the earth, we rise and we fall,
Stone by stone, we conquer it all.

In the moonlit night, shadows will dance,
Carved by the light, we take our chance.
Hearts intertwined, we face the unknown,
Together we stand, stone by stone.

At the journey's end, what have we sown?
Life's fragile moments, carefully grown.
With each cherished memory, we brightly gleam,
For love is the mortar of our dream.

The Architect's Dream

Blueprints unfold in a whispering breeze,
Visions of grandeur sway with the trees.
Lines of creation, guiding the way,
Dreams of tomorrow, igniting the day.

Vaulted ceilings reach for the stars,
While shadows of doubt hide behind bars.
With hammer and nails, we sculpt our fate,
In the architect's dream, we patiently wait.

Columns of strength rising so high,
Embracing the warmth of a dawn sky.
Every structure built, a piece of our soul,
In the architect's vision, we find our goal.

From sketches to stone, our hopes create,
A legacy strong, we dare not wait.
With every heartbeat, the vision is clear,
For in the architect's dream, we have no fear.

Foundations of Thought

Beneath the surface, quiet dreams lie,
Foundations of thought, reaching for the sky.
In the stillness, ideas collide,
Waves of insight, like the ocean tide.

Epiphanies spark in the depth of the night,
Illuminating paths with their brilliant light.
Each thought a stone, we gather with care,
Building a castle, a fortress to share.

Voices of wisdom echo through time,
In the chambers of mind, they resonate, chime.
With patience we breathe, ideas take flight,
Foundations of thought, soaring into the light.

Harvesting dreams, we find our own way,
In the garden of learning, we choose to stay.
For knowledge is strength, a treasure we seek,
Foundations of thought, in silence, we speak.

Bricks of Emotion

Layered in love, we build with our hearts,
Bricks of emotion, each one imparts.
Joy and sorrow, woven in time,
Creating a structure, a rhythm, a rhyme.

From laughter to tears, we gather them near,
Bricks of emotion, both salty and clear.
With every heartbeat, we lay them down,
A fortress of feelings, our shelter, our crown.

Strength in connection, we rise from the fall,
Each brick a story, a testament, a call.
In the warmth of each hug, the spark in the eye,
Bricks of emotion, as days whisper by.

As the seasons change, they weather and bend,
Still standing strong, they never will end.
For love is the mortar, a bond we can't sever,
Building forever, with bricks of endeavor.

Milton Keynes UK
Ingram Content Group UK Ltd.
UKHW032316121024
449481UK00011B/330